Barefoot Books

CONSTELLATIONS

STORIES IN THE STARS

written by **Anne Jankeliowitch**
illustrated by **Sarah Andreacchio**

reviewed & edited by Dr. Carie Cardamone, PhD
translated by Lisa Rosinsky

STAR CHART

Imagine drawing lines in the sky to connect stars into the shape of a dog, or a bear, or a swan. That's called a **constellation**!

In ancient times, people saw shapes in groups of stars and named them after the heroes of their stories. The constellations in this book are named after characters from ancient Greek mythology, but throughout history, cultures all over the world have seen their own stories in the stars. Today, the International Astronomical Union (IAU) recognizes eighty-eight constellations. We will explore fifteen of them in this book.

This map shows forty-one constellations visible from the Northern Hemisphere. Even though our view of the night sky shifts with the seasons, the position of the constellations relative to one another does not change. So if you find the Big Dipper or Orion (the brightest constellations), you can use those groups of stars to locate other stars nearby.

Make sure you keep your star chart out as you read ahead!

Note: **Fully capitalized names are constellations and names in uppercase/lowercase are individual stars.**

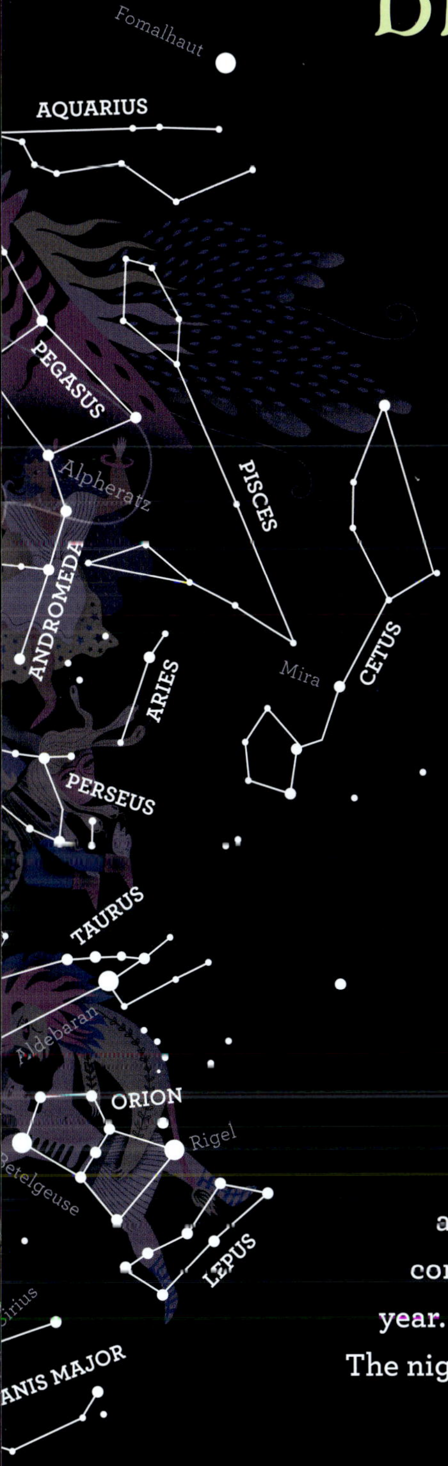

BEFORE GOING STARGAZING...

Q: How far away are the stars?

A: Space is so enormous that it is measured in a unit called a **light-year** — the distance light can travel in one year. Light travels at a speed of 186,282 miles per second (300,000 km/s). Find that hard to imagine? Think about this: on average, it takes only thirteen minutes for light to travel from Earth to Mars. If a high-speed metro train could make the same journey, it would take more than eighty-five years! So how far can light travel in a year? One light-year equals 5.8 trillion miles (9.4 trillion km).

Q: Are all the stars the same distance away from us?

A: No, some stars are closer to us while others are further away. While it might look like constellations are flat, they are actually three-dimensional. The lines that connect the stars into constellations are imaginary.

Q: Does the night sky always look the same?

A: Again, no. Our view of the stars changes throughout the night. Like the Sun, the stars appear to rise in the east and set in the west due to the Earth's rotation on its **axis** (an imaginary line around which Earth rotates). The night sky also changes from one season to the next. Some constellations close to the North Star are visible throughout the year. These are called **circumpolar constellations**. Other constellations that are lower on the horizon are only visible at certain times of the year. The constellations in this book are only visible in the Northern Hemisphere. The night sky looks different from the Southern Hemisphere!

but are actually very far away. Others appear motionless but are in fact moving incredibly fast. Here are some things you might see while stargazing, from closest to furthest away.

BIRDS AND BATS

Distance: a few feet/m
Speed: up to 25 mph (40 km/h)

At night, the sky becomes the realm of nocturnal birds of prey. You might spot the shadow of an owl or nighthawk as it swoops past. If you see something flying faster, with lots of acrobatic twists and turns, that might be a bat!

PLANES

Distance: approx. 7.4 mi (12 km)
Speed: 560 mph (900 km/h)

If you see a moving, blinking dot and hear the roar of an engine, you've spotted a plane. If it's flying too high to be heard, you might still be able to identify it by its blinking green and red lights. You can watch planes cross the entire sky (unless they go behind a cloud). A plane might look no larger than a star — can you imagine that 500 people could be up there in that tiny point of light?

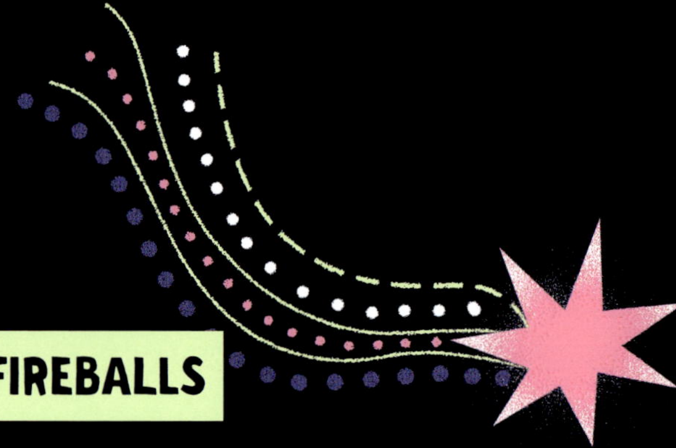

FIREBALLS

Distance: 18–50 mi (30–80 km), or sometimes as close as 6 mi (10 km)
Speed: approx. 35,000 mph (57,000 km/h) or 10 miles per second (16 km/s)

If you see an extra-bright shooting star that seems to cross the entire sky, it's probably an extra-large meteor called a **fireball**. If a fireball doesn't completely disintegrate in the atmosphere, it becomes a **meteorite** — a rocky fragment from space that crashes onto the Earth's surface, forming a crater. It's rare to find a meteorite on the ground, but you won't miss a fireball if it crosses the sky while you're watching!

SHOOTING STARS

Distance: 35–75 miles (60–120 km)
Speed: approx. 155,000 mph (250,000 km/h) or 43 mi per second (70 km/s)

Earth is surrounded by a protective layer of gas called the **atmosphere**. If an object hurtles towards us from space, it hits this protective shield at a very high speed. Friction with the gases in the atmosphere causes the object to heat up so much that it burns. As it falls through the atmosphere, it creates a glowing trail that lasts for a few seconds before it burns up completely. These objects are called **meteors**, or shooting stars.

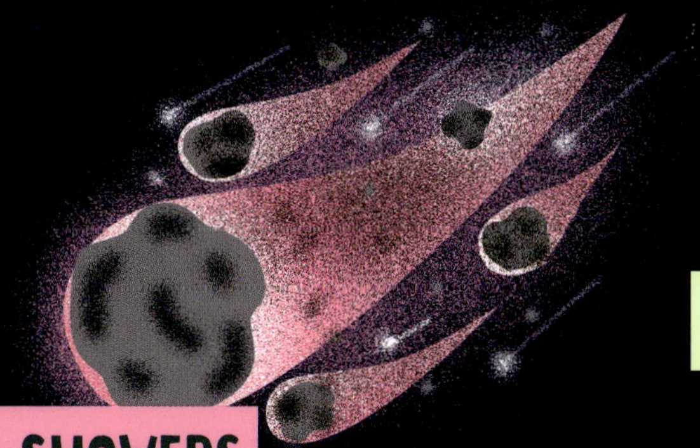

METEOR SHOWERS

When Earth crosses the path of a comet orbiting the Sun, we pass through the trail of dust and debris the comet leaves behind. These particles are about the size of grains of sand. When they enter our atmosphere, they turn into meteors, and what we see from Earth is a shower of shooting stars that appear to all come from the same area of the sky. If you watch a meteor shower, you could see a hundred shooting stars in just one hour!

Earth passes through certain comets on the same dates each year, so we know when those meteor showers will take place. They are named for constellations that appear nearby. The best-known meteor shower is the Perseids, on August 11. You can also observe the Orionids, which originate from debris left behind by Halley's Comet (October 21); the Geminids (December 13); or the Ursids (December 22).

UFOs?

Distance: unknown
Speed: unknown

Unidentified flying objects (UFOs) are alien spaceships. They are also called flying saucers. If you see one, go and tell an adult right away . . .

That's just a joke — nobody has ever been able to prove that UFOs (or aliens!) really exist outside of stories. But as **astronomers** build stronger telescopes to explore space, they continue to find more faraway planets where they can search for signs of life. If we live in an infinite universe, it is entirely possible that life exists somewhere else besides Earth. But where would it be, and what would it look like? Nobody knows the answers. What do you think?

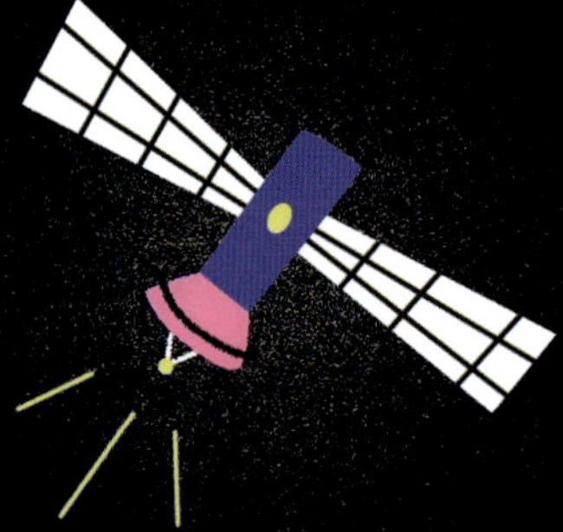

SATELLITES

Distance: 120–620 mi (200–1,000 km)
Speed: approx. 15,500 mph (25,000 km/h)
or 4 miles per second (7 km/s)

A **satellite** is any object that orbits (travels around) another object. Artificial satellites are made by people and sent into space to orbit Earth, while natural satellites, such as the Moon, orbit planets. Satellites are visible to the naked eye because they reflect the Sun's rays, much like a mirror.

Artificial satellites can sometimes be mistaken for airplane lights. When watching one move among the stars, it may slowly disappear as it enters Earth's shadow. If a satellite appears to blink, it is rotating and reflecting sunlight at different angles. Thousands of artificial satellites orbit Earth today, and they are used for communication, weather forecasting, scientific research, photography, and GPS.

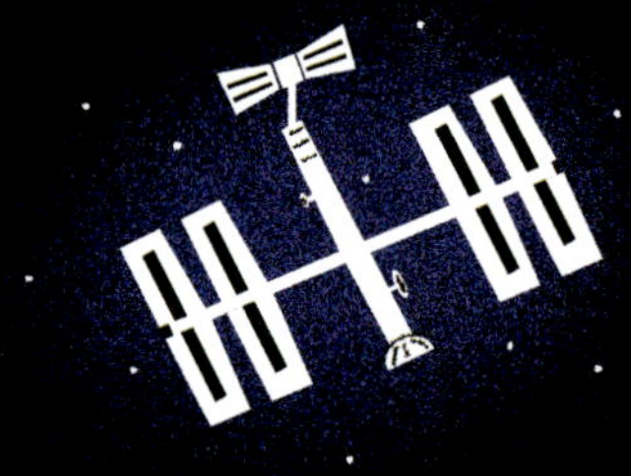

THE INTERNATIONAL SPACE STATION (ISS)

Distance: 250 mi (400 km)
Speed: 17,000 mph (27,700 km/h)
or 5 miles per second (7.7 km/s)

The **ISS** is a space laboratory for scientific research, and it has room for up to six astronauts to live and work there. It was launched into orbit in 1998. Astronauts travel there on a space shuttle, and the trip takes about six hours. Some astronauts stay up there for several months at a time!

With its large solar panels reflecting the Sun's rays, the ISS is the brightest of all artificial satellites. From Earth, the station looks like a bright dot moving across the starry sky for three to four minutes. You can look online to find out when the ISS will be visible in the sky where you live.

THE MOON

Distance: 240,000 mi (384,000 km)

Six times smaller than Earth, the **Moon** is our natural satellite. It takes twenty-nine days (roughly one month) to orbit our planet.

We always see the same side of the Moon because it rotates on its axis at the same rate as it revolves around the Earth. The Moon does not produce its own light. It looks like it is shining because it reflects the light of the Sun.

As the Moon revolves around the Earth, it sometimes travels into Earth's shadow. This is why we see the Moon move through a cycle from full moon, to gibbous, to quarter, to crescent, to new moon (when we can no longer see it) and back again.

When the Moon is full, you might be able to see its "dark spots," which are seas of ancient cooled lava.

PLANETS

Distance:
Venus: approx. 50 million mi (80 million km)
Mars: approx. 150 million mi (240 million km)
Jupiter: approx. 500 million mi (800 million km)
Saturn: approx. 1 billion mi (1.5 billion km)

Earth is one of eight planets in our solar system. Each planet revolves around the Sun at a different speed and on a different orbital path. Venus, Mars, Jupiter, and Saturn are close enough to Earth that we can see them in the night sky. Unlike stars, they shine but do not twinkle. Like satellites, they reflect the rays of the Sun. Venus is sometimes called the Morning Star or Evening Star because it is easiest to spot at sunrise and sunset.

THE SHEPHERD'S STAR

Distance: approx. 50 million mi (80 million km)

Venus is also called the Shepherd's Star. Because it is visible at dawn and dusk, it signals to shepherds when to take their flocks out to pasture or bring them back home. It is not the same as the North Star, which is in an entirely different part of the sky. In fact, the "North Star" is not one single star — rather, it is the title for whichever star can be found along Earth's rotational axis. And of course Venus is not a star at all — it is a planet! The clouds of gas surrounding it reflect sunlight very well, making it appear bright in the sky, almost like a star.

COMETS

**Measurements from Halley's Comet (1986)*
Distance: approx. 90 million mi (150 million km)
Speed: approx. 100,000 mph (180,000 km/h) or 30 miles per second (50 km/s)

Comets are small balls of ice and dust that orbit the Sun, originally formed at the same time as the planets in our solar system. The largest are only 6 miles (10 km) wide, which is tiny compared to the vastness of outer space! As a comet orbits, the Sun's heat turns its ice into gas, which mixes with dust to form a "tail" that stretches for millions of mi/km. Tiny comets are visible to us in the night sky because of these tails. It is rare to spot a comet, but some do pass Earth regularly: Halley's Comet travels past us every seventy-six years. It will next be visible in the year 2061!

STARS

There's no need to search for stars in the night sky — they're everywhere! The stars we can see are all part of our galaxy, the Milky Way. Our galaxy contains more than 100 billion stars, though only 6,000 are visible to the naked eye (and far fewer are visible from any single location on Earth). Stars are very hot balls of gas that come in a wide range of ages, sizes, temperatures, etc. They make energy and light, which is why they appear to twinkle in the night sky. The star closest to us is the Sun, which shines so brightly it gives us daylight!

SIRIUS

Distance: 8 light-years

To spot Sirius, look for the brightest star in the night sky! Follow the line of Orion's Belt and it will lead you to Sirius in the constellation Canis Major. It's the main star of the constellation Canis Major, which you can find by looking downwards from Orion's Belt. Its bluish-white light shines as brightly as twenty of our Suns combined, even though it is only about twice the size of our Sun. Sirius is one of the closest stars to Earth.

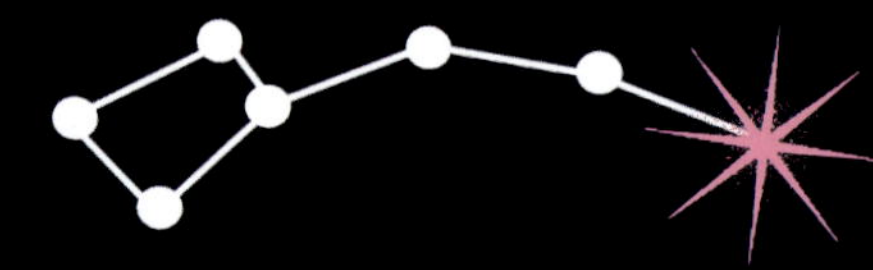

THE NORTH STAR

Distance: 430 light-years

You can find the North Star, also called Polaris, at the end of the Little Dipper's handle. It's not the brightest star in the sky, but it is special for another reason: it appears stationary, and all the other stars seem to revolve around it throughout the night. This is because it is aligned with Earth's axis of rotation. In other words, if you stood at the North Pole, the North Star would be directly above you all night long. You can use it to orient yourself at night without a compass or GPS, and it has guided explorers and navigators for centuries. If you imagine a straight line extending from the North Star down to Earth, the point where that line meets the horizon is true north.

THE MILKY WAY

Scientists estimate there are 50 billion galaxies in the universe. We live in a galaxy called **the Milky Way**, made of gas, dust, and 100 billion stars. The Milky Way is a spinning spiral shape that measures 100,000 light-years across. Imagine that you could stand at one end of the galaxy while a friend pointed a flashlight at you from the other end. You would have to wait 100,000 years to see that light! Earth and the seven other planets in our solar system, along with the Sun, are located in one of the Milky Way's spiral arms, 27,000 light-years from the middle of the galaxy. On a clear night, you can see the Milky Way as a large white band across the sky.

GALAXIES

Even the closest nearby galaxies to the Milky Way are so far away that you would need a telescope to see most of them. Only one is visible to the naked eye: the Andromeda Galaxy. It has 200 billion stars and is named after the constellation Andromeda because that is the area of the sky in which it appears. We might call it "close" to us, but it's still 2.5 million light-years away. That means that when you spot it in the night sky, you are seeing light that left the Andromeda Galaxy 2.5 million years ago — long before humans even existed.

Ursa Major
Great Bear

Ursa Major is one of the most famous constellations. Its name is Latin for "Great Bear." It was mapped by Greco-Roman astronomer Ptolemy around two thousand years ago. Seven main stars in the back and tail of the bear form a smaller constellation called "the Saucepan" by the French, "the Plough" by the English, or "the Big Dipper" by Americans.

Look for 7 bright stars to find the constellation

Best time to look: All year!

✶ If you stare at the middle star of the bear's "tail," you might think you see two stars very close together. These are called Mizar and Alcor. In reality, they are very far apart from each other, but they look almost perfectly aligned from our perspective.

✶ Two stars form the edge of the dipper across from the handle. Imagine a line connecting them, and then extend that line about five times further from the top of the Saucepan. That's where you'll find the North Star!

Bear or Nymph?

In Greek mythology, there was once a beautiful nymph named Callisto. Zeus, the king of all the gods, fell in love with her, and together they had a son named Arcas. When Zeus's wife, Hera, found out, she went wild with jealousy. Hera asked Artemis, goddess of the hunt, to turn Callisto into a bear. As a bear, poor Callisto fled to live in the mountains. Finally, to protect Callisto and Arcas, Zeus placed them in the sky as constellations. He positioned them close to the North Star so that he could watch over them. Callisto became Ursa Major. Read on to learn about Arcas's fate . . .

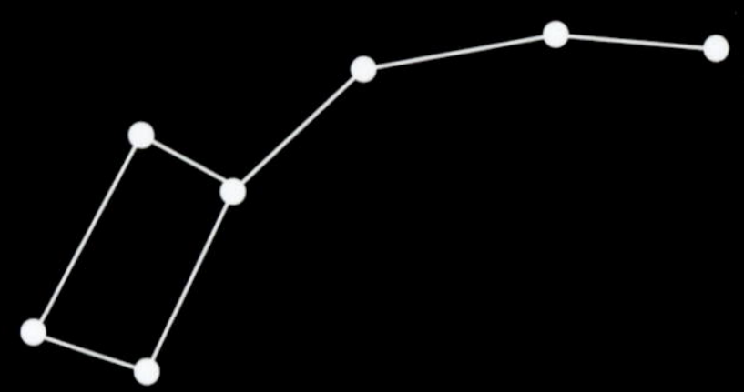

Ursa Minor
Little Bear

Ursa Minor, also called "Little Bear" or "the Little Dipper," looks like Ursa Major but smaller and reversed. To find it, look for the Big Dipper in Ursa Major. The two stars at the edge of the saucepan point to the North Star, which marks the end of the Little Dipper's handle.

Look for 7 bright stars to find the constellation

Best time to look: All year!

The Little Dipper is not very bright. The North Star is the brightest star in the constellation and is useful for finding it. With a shape and position similar to the Big Dipper, the Little Dipper looks a bit like a ladle dipped in a pot! But you can only see this image in the sky in the autumn and early winter. By springtime, the Big Dipper appears above the Little Dipper — in other words, with the pot above the ladle.

A Hunter Among the Stars

Arcas, the son of Callisto, grew up in a village far from his mother. He became a strong, skilled archer. One day, when he was hunting in the mountains, he took aim with his bow and arrow at a beautiful bear. Zeus was watching and realized that Arcas was about to unknowingly kill his own mother, who had been transformed into a bear. To prevent this tragedy, Zeus turned Arcas into a smaller bear. Then Zeus grabbed both bears by their tails and threw them into the sky, stretching their tails as he turned them into constellations. The myth says that this is why their tails are so long.

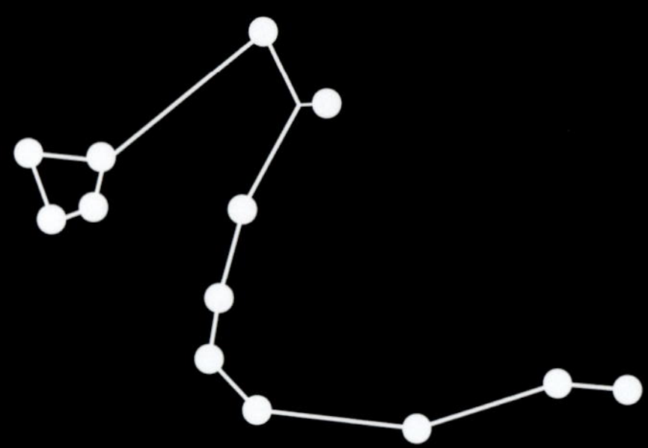

DRACO THE DRAGON

Find the tail of Draco, which means "dragon," winding its way between Ursa Major and Ursa Minor. Draco wraps around Ursa Minor, then makes a sharp turn to form an "S" shape. This large constellation only shines faintly and does not contain any especially bright stars, but its curving shape makes it easy to find.

Look for 13 bright stars to find the constellation

Best time to look: June–October

✶ Draco was one of the constellations recorded by the Greco-Roman astronomer Ptolemy, who lived in Alexandria, Egypt, in the second century CE.

✶ As Earth's tilt changes slowly over thousands of years, the North Star changes as well. Five thousand years ago, it was the star Thuban, in the Draco constellation. But 8,000 years from now, the North Star will be Deneb, the brightest star in the Cygnus constellation.

Guardian of the Sky

In one Greco-Roman myth, the hero Jason had to steal a magical golden fleece guarded by a dragon. In another myth, the hero Cadmus had to fight a dragon in order to drink water from a spring in a forest belonging to the god Ares. In many other tales, too, dragons are depicted as fierce guardians of treasure. And this dragon, way up in the sky — what treasure do you think it could be hiding?

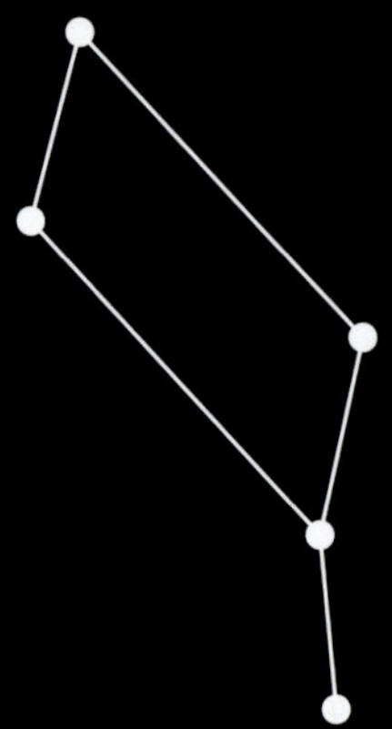

LYRA THE LYRE

The lyre is a small harp with five to eight strings. It was a popular musical instrument in ancient times.

Look for 5 bright stars to find the constellation

Best time to look: May–November

✶ Vega, the brightest star in the Lyra constellation, shines with a bluish glow. Vega is in fact the brightest star in the whole summer sky. It is three times larger than the Sun and fifty times brighter.

Down into the Underworld

In Greek mythology, there once lived a famous musician named Orpheus. When his wife Eurydice died, he was consumed by grief and went to the Underworld to try to bring her back. He played his lyre to charm the ferocious beast guarding the gates of the Underworld and earned the right to bring Eurydice back with him to the land of the living. There was only one condition: until they returned to the surface, he couldn't look at her. But at the very end of the journey, Orpheus couldn't resist turning to look at Eurydice. Orpheus lost his love forever . . . until he died, too, and was reunited with her in the Underworld. As a tribute to Orpheus's musical talent and his sorrow following the loss of Eurydice, his lyre was placed in the sky.

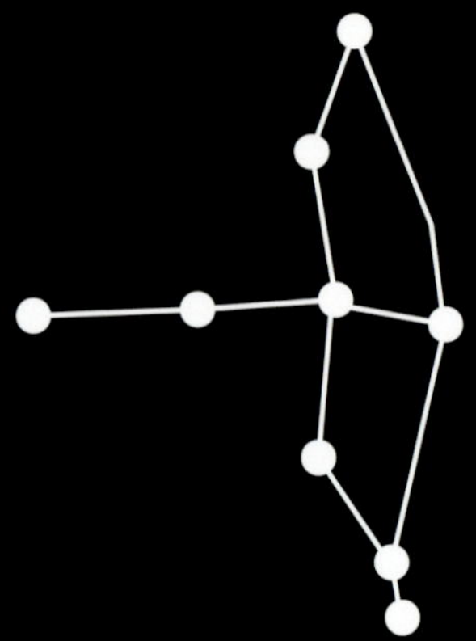

CYGNUS THE SWAN

To find Cygnus in the night sky, first look for the large Summer Triangle, made up of the bright stars Vega, Deneb, and Altair; Deneb marks the tail of Cygnus. The constellation forms a large cross shape known as the Northern Cross, with a line of stars stretching down to Albireo at the swan's head and two stars extending sideways as wings.

Look for 9 bright stars to find the constellation

Best time to look: June–November

✶ Cygnus is a large, bright constellation. The long-necked bird flies towards the south, following the Milky Way, which illuminates the summer sky.

✶ Deneb (Cygnus's tail) is a type of star called a blue supergiant. Its surface has a temperature of around 15,000°F (8,500°C) — this is hotter than the Sun, which is approximately 10,000°F (5,500°C).

Phaethon's Death

One day, Cygnus's best friend, Phaethon, fell into the river Eridanus after crashing the chariot belonging to his father, the sun god. Cygnus dove into the river again and again trying to save his friend, but he could not reach him. Zeus saw his sadness and transformed him into a swan so he could dive deep after his friend. Though Cygnus sacrificed his life as a human, he was able to reach his friend and bring his body back. Zeus placed him among the stars to remember this heroic act.

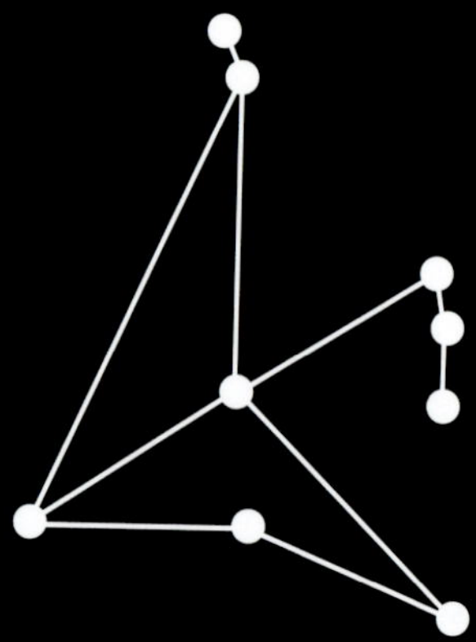

AQUILA THE EAGLE

Aquila lies along the bright band of the Milky Way. Its most prominent star is Altair, which forms part of the Summer Triangle along with Vega and Deneb. Aquila is shaped like a flying eagle, with Altair marking the head and a line of stars extending outward on both sides to form its wings

---

Look for 9 bright stars to find the constellation

Best time to look:
July–October

Altair is part of the Summer Triangle, which is not a constellation. The Summer Triangle is an **asterism**, a group of stars that can help you locate nearby constellations. The Summer Triangle appears high overhead on warm summer evenings and stands out because its three stars are very bright and widely spaced.

The Gods' Cupbearer

Aquila was said to be Zeus's powerful eagle and personal messenger. Zeus sent Aquila to carry a beautiful young man named Ganymede up to Mount Olympus so he could serve wine and food to the gods. Because of Aquila's loyalty and strength, the eagle was placed among the stars. Some also say that the eagle carried Zeus's thunderbolts.

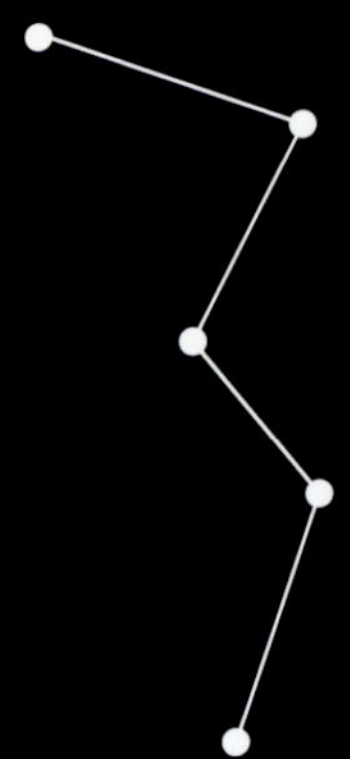

CASSIOPEIA THE QUEEN

To find Cassiopeia in the night sky, look for a distinctive "W" or "M" shape made of five bright stars. This zigzag pattern forms the outline of the constellation and makes it one of the easiest to recognize. Cassiopeia sits opposite Ursa Major (the Big Dipper) across the North Star, Polaris, so if you can find Ursa Major, you can trace a line through its bowl to Polaris and then continue on the other side to spot Cassiopeia.

Look for 5 bright stars to find the constellation

Best time to look: August–January

The brightest star in Cassiopeia is an orange star called Schedar. It is 230 light-years away from us. It might look very small to us, but in reality, it is about 700 times brighter than the Sun and 50 times larger.

Nearby constellations include Cepheus, Andromeda, Perseus, and Pegasus. All are named for characters from the legend of Andromeda.

The Upside-Down Queen

Cassiopeia was a queen of Ethiopia and wife to King Cepheus. Together they had a daughter named Andromeda. Cassiopeia was quite vain and declared that she and Andromeda were more beautiful than the sea nymphs known as the Nereids. This angered Poseidon, the god of the sea, who decided that Cassiopeia's vanity should be punished. This is how she found herself tied to her throne, revolving around the North Pole — and at certain times of the year, hanging upside down in a very unroyal posture.

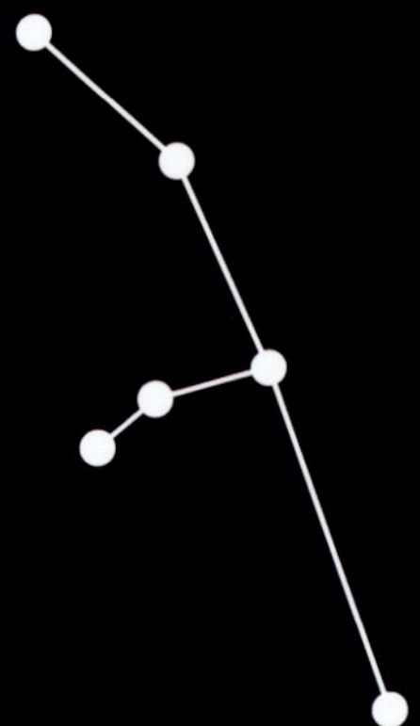

ANDROMEDA THE CHAINED LADY

To find Andromeda, near Cassiopeia, identify three bright stars in a straight line, which will help lead you to the other three stars of the constellation.

Look for 6 bright stars to find the constellation

Best time to look: August–January

In this constellation, you'll find the furthest celestial object visible to the naked eye: the Andromeda Galaxy, more than 2.5 million light-years away from us. It looks like a small, fuzzy oval near Mirach (the star in the middle of the constellation). Though it's hard to imagine, some of the stars you see shining brightly in the Andromeda Galaxy may already be extinct. But we will still be able to see them in the sky until the last rays of light they emitted have finished their journey to us — in two million years!

A Hero Just in Time

Princess Andromeda was the daughter of Queen Cassiopeia and King Cepheus. Cassiopeia had angered the sea god Poseidon, and as punishment, Poseidon sent a sea monster, Cetus, to attack the kingdom. An oracle declared that the only way to save the land was to sacrifice Andromeda, so she was chained to a rock by the sea. Perseus, on his way home after battling an evil witch named Medusa — who could turn her enemies to stone with a single glance — came to Andromeda's rescue. Perseus defeated Medusa by cutting off her head, which retained her magical powers. With Medusa's head, Perseus was able to turn Cetus into stone just as it was about to attack Andromeda.

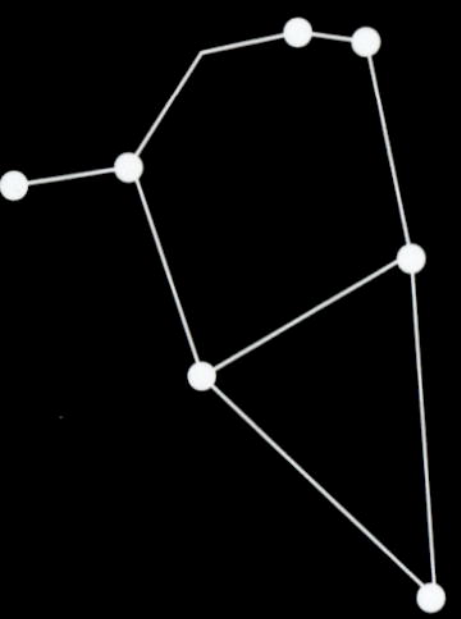

CEPHEUS THE KING

Cepheus looks like an upside-down house with a pointy roof. This constellation, which is not very bright, can be found between Cassiopeia and Ursa Minor. The peak of its "roof" points towards the North Star.

Look for 7 bright stars to find the constellation

Best time to look: August–January

* Cepheus's brightest star is at the lower right corner of the house. It is called Alderamin.

* Although it is hard to see with the naked eye, many stars in the night sky vary in brightness. In 1784, an astronomer discovered that Delta Cephei (near the top left corner of the house, and the one furthest out) gets brighter and then dimmer over a matter of days. Today an entire class of stars, called **Cepheids**, are named after this star.

A Father's Love

Cepheus was the king of an ancient kingdom in Northern Africa. When the hero Perseus saved Cepheus's daughter Andromeda from a sea monster, Cepheus gave his blessing for Perseus and Andromeda to marry. They had a son, Perses, and Cepheus made Perses his heir. Cepheus was placed among the stars with his wife Cassiopeia and his daughter Andromeda.

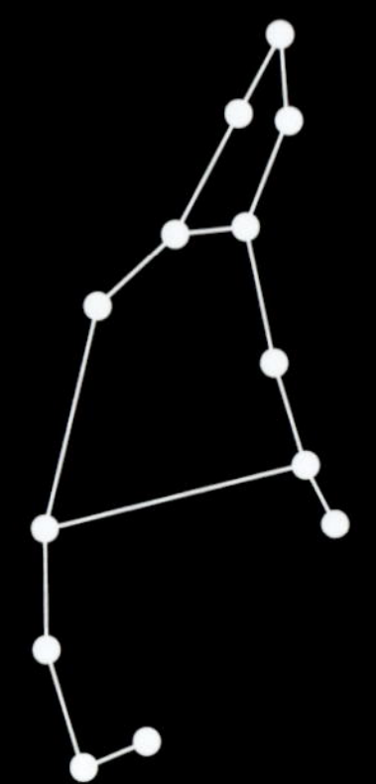

PERSEUS THE HERO

This bright constellation lies just below Cassiopeia, appearing as a curved chain of stars stretching away from Cassiopeia. It is also near Andromeda.

Look for 13 bright stars to find the constellation

Best time to look: November–March

✶ Mirfak, the brightest star in Perseus, is a yellow supergiant. About 500 light-years away from us, it is hotter and much larger than the Sun.

✶ Look for a round, hazy patch halfway between the peaks of Perseus and Cassiopeia. These are two star clusters, each containing more than 300 stars. You can see them easily with binoculars.

✶ Each year around August 12, you can observe the Perseids, a meteor shower that appears to come from the constellation of Perseus. These meteors are fragments of dust from the Swift–Tuttle comet.

The Mirror Trick

Medusa was one of the three **Gorgons** — evil creatures that turned anyone they looked at into stone. She was defeated by a hero named Perseus, son of the god Zeus and the princess Danaë. Since Perseus could not look directly at Medusa without being turned to stone, he came up with a clever trick. Looking only at her reflection in the surface of his shield, which was highly polished so it could be used as a mirror, he was able to chase her down and cut off her head.

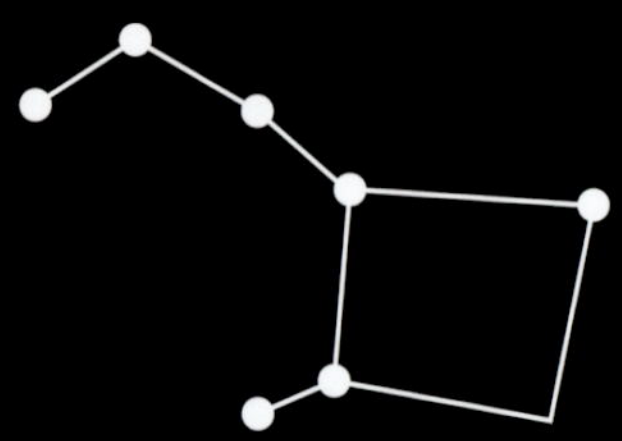

PEGASUS THE WINGED HORSE

To find Pegasus in the night sky, look for the large square of four bright stars. From a corner of the square, a line of fainter stars extends outwards to form the horse's neck and head. Near Cassiopeia and directly connected to Andromeda, this constellation is easily findable in the dark sky because it lies outside the Milky Way.

Look for 8 bright stars to find the constellation

Best time to look: August–January

✶ Opposite Alpheratz and diagonally across the sky, you will find Markab, the third brightest star in Pegasus. It forms the base of the horse's neck. Markab is a subgiant, hotter and larger than the Sun. Scheat, at the bottom left of the square, is a red giant that is cooler than the Sun and shines with an orange glow.

✶ One of the stars in Pegasus is called 51 Pegasi, which is famous for being the first Sun-like star found to host an **exoplanet** (a planet outside our solar system). It looks like a twin of our Sun.

A Horse in the Air

Pegasus is a horse with wings! He sprang from Medusa's body right after Perseus killed her. Perseus jumped onto Pegasus's back, and they flew to rescue Andromeda from the sea monster Cetus. Following these adventures, Perseus brought Pegasus to Mount Olympus. There, the winged horse received a special job: bringing bolts of lightning and thunder to Zeus, king of the gods.

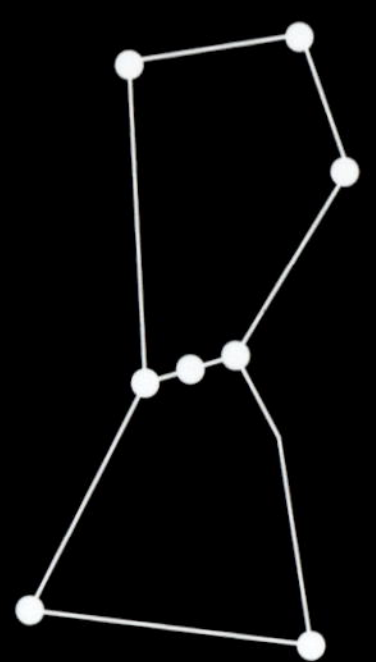

ORION THE HUNTER

Orion is a very bright constellation in the winter night sky. It rises near the southeast horizon. You can easily recognize its hourglass shape, with three stars in a diagonal line at the narrow middle.

Look for 8 bright stars to find the constellation

Best time to look: December–March

✶ Betelgeuse and Rigel are two of the brightest and most prominent stars in Orion at the top left and bottom right, respectively. To the right, though not part of the core stars that form the constellation, you can find stars in a circle that form his "shield."

✶ The **Orion Nebula** (also called M42) is a vast cloud of gas and dust, where new stars are currently being born. It is 1,500 light years away from us and visible to the naked eye as a hazy patch in the "sword" below Orion's Belt.

Sworn Enemies

Orion was a great hunter who boasted that he could conquer any beast, no matter how fierce. The goddess Hera wanted to teach Orion a lesson for being so proud. So she sent a scorpion, Scorpius, after him. Scorpius bit Orion and injected its deadly venom. Zeus turned Orion into a constellation in memory of his greatness as a hunter. Meanwhile, Hera sent Scorpius into the sky as well, to thank it for its loyal service to her. But the gods placed the two of them in positions where they would never cross paths again: when Orion rises in the east, Scorpius sets in the west.

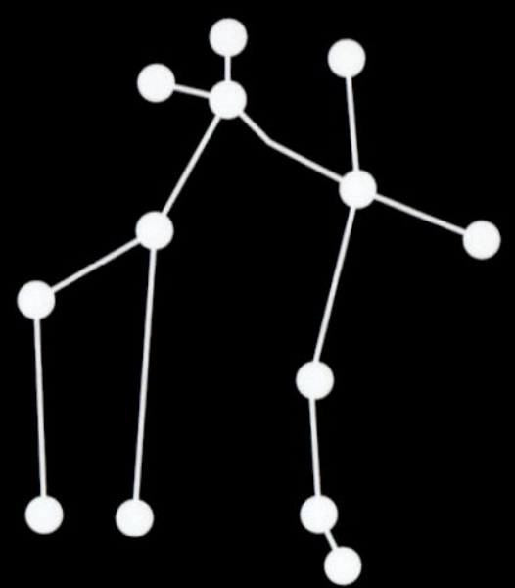

GEMINI THE TWINS

Look to the left of Orion to find the twins, Gemini. Two bright stars, Castor and Pollux, mark the heads of the twin brothers. From the heads, fainter stars extend downwards to form their bodies.

Look for 13 bright stars to find the constellation

Best time to look: December–May

✶ Pollux marks the head of the "twin" on the left. It is a giant, orange-glowing star that is cooler than the Sun and about 35 light-years away from us.

✶ Castor marks the head of the "twin" on the right and looks similar to Pollux to the naked eye. But if you look through a small telescope, you'll be surprised! Castor is not really a single star, but a system of six stars orbiting around each other.

Brothers of the Sky

Castor and Pollux were twin brothers. Their mother was the nymph Leda and their father was Zeus. Only one of the brothers, Pollux, inherited his father's immortality. Castor, on the other hand, was born without this gift. But they loved each other so much that when Castor died, Pollux begged Zeus to let him rejoin his brother. According to the legend, his father granted his wish, and this is why they remain side by side in the night sky.

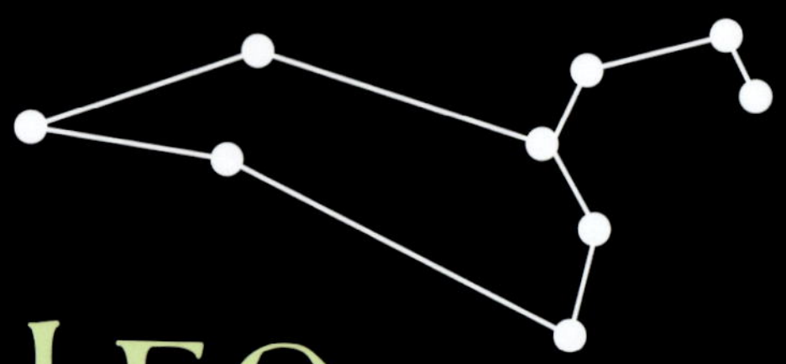

LEO THE LION

Find the two stars that form the edge of Ursa Major, on the handle side. Now extend the line connecting them downwards towards a bright star. That's Regulus, the brightest star in Leo. Like Gemini, Leo is one of the constellations of the **Zodiac**, a group of twelve constellations that make up the path the sun takes across the sky each year.

Look for 9 bright stars to find the constellation

Best time to look:
February–June

✳ The ancient Greeks thought this constellation looked like a lion, but other cultures around the world have seen different pictures in these stars. For the Taurepang people of Brazil, it represents their god of lightning and thunder. The ancient people of Siberia saw a constellation in the shape of a sleeping woman. You might even think this constellation looks a bit like a coat hanger!

✳ The Leonids are an annual meteor shower in mid-November, featuring bright meteors and fireballs that appear to radiate from the constellation Leo. These meteors and fireballs are debris from the Tempel-Tuttle Comet, which is named after the astronomers who discovered it.

A Lion with Tough Skin

In Greek mythology, a hero named Hercules was given twelve impossible tasks to complete. The first was to kill a fierce lion that was attacking people in a place called Nemea. Hercules discovered that the lion's hide could not be pierced, and his arrows bounced right off without doing any harm. Ultimately, Hercules managed to defeat the lion by forcing it to turn its own claws against itself.

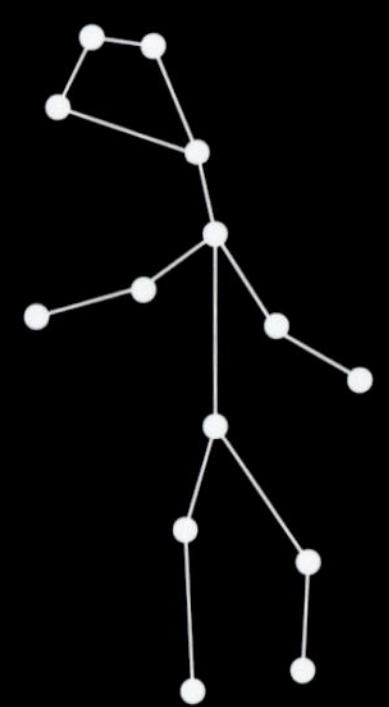

VIRGO THE MAIDEN

Virgo is another constellation of the Zodiac. To find it, look for the slightly curved handle of Ursa Major. If you extend this curving line, you will find the bright star Arcturus, in the constellation Boötes. Then, if you continue along that same arc – almost like continuing a half-circle – you'll reach Spica, one of the central stars in Virgo. The distance from Arcturus to Spica is roughly the same as the distance from the end of the Big Dipper's handle to Arcturus.

Look for 14 bright stars to find the constellation

Best time to look:
April–June

- Spica, the brightest star in Virgo, symbolizes an ear of wheat. It is a white star, about 250 light-years away from us, that is even larger and hotter than the Sun.
- You need a telescope to see it, but in the northern part of this constellation, there is a cluster of several thousand galaxies. This cluster is located 55 million light-years away from us.

A Celestial Escape

Virgo represents the scales of justice and Astraea, the goddess of justice. According to Greek mythology, she was the last of the **immortals** (gods and certain divine beings who live forever) to live among humans on Earth. When she finally decided that humans were too imperfect and corrupt, she returned to Mount Olympus, and Zeus offered her a special place in the heavens.

Barefoot Books
23 Bradford Street, 2nd Floor
Concord, MA 01742

Barefoot Books
40-50 Tottenham Street
London, W1T 4RN

First published in France as *Constellations* © De La Martinière Jeunesse, 2015
Translated by Lisa Rosinsky, Barefoot Books

First published in the United States of America by Barefoot Books, Inc
and in Great Britain by Barefoot Books, Ltd in 2026

Graphic design by Meaghan Elyse Lueck, Barefoot Books
Edited by Erin Lueck and Andrea Pérez, Barefoot Books
Reproduction by Bright Arts, Hong Kong
Printed in Heshan, Guangdong, China. May 2026
For safety queries, contact *productsafety@barefootbooks.com*
This book was typeset in Archer Pro, Azola La, and Graphen
The illustrations were prepared digitally

Hardback ISBN 979-8-89859-163-2
E-book ISBN 979-8-89859-193-9

British Cataloguing-in-Publication Data:
a catalogue record for this book is available from the British Library

Library of Congress Cataloging-in-Publication Data
is available upon request under LCCN 2026934198

1 3 5 7 9 8 6 4 2

Barefoot Books

step inside a story

At Barefoot Books, we celebrate art and story that opens the hearts and minds of children from all walks of life, focusing on themes that encourage independence of spirit, enthusiasm for learning and respect for the world's diversity. The welfare of our children is dependent on the welfare of the planet, so we constantly strive to reduce our environmental impact. Playful, beautiful and created to last a lifetime, our products combine the best of the present with the best of the past to educate our children as the caretakers of tomorrow.

www.barefootbooks.com

Anne Jankeliowitch is an environmental engineer and children's book author. She has dedicated herself to nature conservation, in France and abroad, for the WWF and Greenpeace. She is a regular contributor to books on the natural world, notably in collaboration with the GoodPlanet foundation.

Sarah Andreacchio lives in France, where she illustrates everything from books to games and textiles to stationery. She has a passion for old books and also enjoys making things and listening to music. Sarah has worked for a large number of publishers and other clients throughout Europe.